THE

Pocket Cathedral

❖ A COLLECTION OF PRAYERS ❖

FARRELL MASON

THE Pocket Cathedral

A COLLECTION OF PRAYERS

FARRELL MASON

Other books by Farrell Mason:

Alma Gloria and the Olive Tree

The Angel and the Raven

**Weekly spiritual meditations
at www.breadandhoneyblog.net**

Copyright © 2016 by Farrell Mason
All rights reserved.
Text design: Circa Design
Cover design: Anouska Ricard
Printed in the United States of America
ISBN: 978-0-692-79309-1

This is my love letter to:

Charlie, Belle, Elise, Rose, Percy and Finn.

And my David.

In these words I give you my heart.

My greatest prayer is that you would take God's hand and set out on your own adventure. Always walk toward love, never give up on hope and trust that God will see you through to the other side.

And to Lovey: Everything that I do is marked by your love.

Prologue

Imagine experiencing a "cathedral" moment in the midst of
the busyness of your ordinary day. Slip through the beautiful,
carved, open door. The incense tickles, the bejeweled light
of a rose window above casts a perfect halo above your
head, and a sea of glowing candles calms your restless spirit.
Whisper a prayer, meditate on a familiar psalm or just have a
heart-to-heart with God. Suddenly, ordinary time is elevated. It
becomes sacred.

In the Middle Ages, it was en vogue for gentlemen and ladies,
as well as monks, priests and nuns to secret a miniature book
of prayers into one's coat pocket, habit or silk purse, and
even to bind one fashionably around a slender wrist or velvet
belt loop. Mirroring the splendor of the gothic cathedrals of
the day, these highly decorative missals were full of exquisite
prayers surrounded by gilt illuminations, painted images
and jewels. Not only were they miniature works of art, but
they encouraged spiritual reflection, prayer and inner peace
during the ordinary ministrations of one's day.

The pocket cathedrals originated from the medieval monastic
tradition of the Divine Service or Praying the Hours. A
monk's day was divided into seven sacred wedges of prayer,
beginning with a dawn prayer (Lauds) and finishing with
an evening prayer (Vespers or "the Lighting of the Lamps").
Prayer became this beautiful vehicle to sanctify time, keep the
heart focused on God throughout one's day and experience a
breath of holiness—even transcendence—on this side of the
mystical boundary.

Fourteen years ago, an envelope appeared in my New York
City apartment mail slot. Inside, written in a woman's cursive
scroll, was the gift of this special prayer for me at a crossroads
moment.

As you go through this day, know that I am gently
protecting you. I am as near to you as your breath, as close
to you as your heartbeat. I can see the fragile state of your
emotions. I know how close to the surface your tender
feelings are. I am aware that the wick of your spirit's inner
light is flickering in the winds of your dilemma. But you
are my child, and I am on your side today. I will hold you
in my love until you are strong again. Do not be troubled
or afraid. Do not strive in your own strength, but lean into
my love. Be strengthened by my spirit.
Find comfort in my mercy.
Your shield and defender,
God

In this prayer, I found the tender voice of the cosmic
presence that I always knew intuitively I was connected to,
belonged to in a supernatural way and was loved by beyond
my understanding. I carried that prayer with me every day
to the hospital when my son was being treated for cancer. It
became permanently etched on my heart. Then I began to
write my own prayers and slip them into envelopes to family,
friends, even strangers whom I knew were in need of a word
of hope. It is quite beautiful how prayer mystically binds us
to God and to one another.

This collection of prayers reflect the quiet moments of
my inmost self, where my spirit resides. I find I'm never
as real as when I become vulnerable before my God. It did
not take long in this life for me to realize that the temporal
world ultimately cannot handle my questions, burdens, fears
and doubts. Only God can cover me in the wrappings of
supernatural peace and give me the courage, the wisdom and
the hope for another day.

For me, prayer is a gentle tugging on that invisible thread that connects my soul to the Mysterious One that created and called me into being. It is less about the perfect words and more about discovering who I am, who God is and what I believe.

I especially love the words of the French philosopher Pierre Teilhard de Chardin: "We are not human beings having a spiritual experience. We are spiritual beings having a human experience."

Prayer is the language of our souls.

True prayer requires a leap. To close your eyes, open your heart and trust your most vulnerable and secret self to something unseen and infinite, wildly beyond the imagination, cosmic on an immeasurable scale, intimate in the most divine way and beautifully holy is, by definition, a leap of faith. And yet I believe it is the secret to experiencing, if only for a breath, what it is to find oneself tucked safe under the divine wings while still roped into the harness of our flesh and bone.

The divine tête-à-tête can be accomplished in a centuries-old candlelit chapel, reading inspired texts, during a silent walk in the woods, moving through a sun salutation, counting the stars in the Big Dipper or at the dangerous edge of despair. Even our tears can silently speak for us. Often prayer happens when we find we have nowhere else to go.

There is no perfect prayer, but a sincere and open heart must be the surest way to capture the Divine's attention.

God will meet us where we are: in church, in the hills of Tennessee, on the streets of Paris; at 60, 8, 41 years old; dark skinned, red, purple; divorced, gay, single, married for over 50 years; happy, sad, frightened, overjoyed, cynical, broken, whole, full or empty. And there is neither judgment nor crazy expectations with God. God knows that most of us are doing our very best to find our way.

More than anything, when we pray, it's our way of confessing that we believe something magnificent, redemptive, loyal and loving is at work in this world and invested in our well-being. We are not alone.

My present-day pocket cathedral is a collection of heart-searching prayers woven gently together by an illumined thread of hope. Carry it on your person to read anytime, anywhere. Lay it at the altar of another's heart and trust God to take care of the rest.

I invite you to stop for just a breath each day, open *The Pocket Cathedral* and whisper a prayer. Elevate an ordinary moment as something special and sacred. Make where you are holy by including God in the conversation of your life. Be less afraid and more assured of God's presence in and around you. Watch how the light streaming through the rose window above and in your heart will suddenly illumine and bend its very rays like wings around you.

Live in hope,
Farrell Mason

NOW FAITH IS THE SUBSTANCE OF THINGS HOPED
FOR, THE EVIDENCE OF THINGS NOT SEEN.

HEBREWS 11:1

od of heaven and earth,

When I close my eyes, slow my breath and ask You to enter in—

I feel the shift in gravity.

You are there.

No longer am I relying on myself and the material
world for my grounding and truth.

But You—The One whose Love never fails.

I ask now that You would peel me back.

Peel back my past: The mistakes, the scars, the hurt and grief,
the doubts and secret fears, until You reach—

A place of holiness inside me.

That part of me drawn to hope, refusing to give into despair,
sees first the goodness in others, and experiences Your
world with a sense of wonder and awe.

If only I could see myself through Your benevolent eyes.

Then maybe I would have more reverence for the path that has
led me to this very moment, honor this sacred vessel of flesh
and bone and the miracle of my lighted soul.

Grace after grace You have shown me.

Help me to see that in every breath something sacred is at stake.

With courage, I will walk forward knowing without knowing

Towards You, with You, and for You.

A holiest amen.

IF YOU BRING FORTH WHAT IS WITHIN YOU, WHAT YOU BRING FORTH WILL SAVE YOU. IF YOU DO NOT BRING FORTH WHAT IS WITHIN YOU, WHAT YOU DO NOT BRING FORTH WILL DESTROY YOU.

GOSPEL OF THOMAS (ATTRIBUTED TO JESUS)

 ivine One,

What would You discover if You gazed inside to
the anatomy of my soul?

Would You see a noble spirit, one that is drawn to hope,
peaceful and not afraid of Your mystery?

Would I be full of faith, trusting in You that all would be well?

Would You feel gentleness and a depth of compassion,
delighting in the corners of my soul where I have set aside my
ego and given wholly over to the needs of another?

If You were to peer into my heart, would it reflect how brave
and resilient I have proven in the face of life's setbacks, because
I knew You were always by my side?

Or would it be darkness on the inside, full of the shadows
of doubt, grief and fear?

Please say I would glow, humbled by the miracle that is my life.

You know me from the inside out.

The truth: I am vulnerable. I hurt. I doubt. I hope.
I yearn for healing and wholeness.

I need You.

Promise that when I speak into the silence, that You will hear the
narrative of my heart and will tenderly reply,

Be still and know that I am your God.

Amen.

TRUE, WHOLE PRAYER IS NOTHING BUT LOVE.

ST. AUGUSTINE

nfinite and Holy One,

When I close my eyes, bow my head and surrender to the moment,

I come to You from the seat of my soul—

That place of my greatest vulnerability and divine potential.

The life odyssey humbles.

I ask pardon for the places in my life
where I have missed the holy mark:

Where I have not loved well enough,

Where my pride has gotten the best of me,

Where I have chosen "I" instead of "Thou."

It's a challenge to listen for Your still, small voice
amidst the clatter noise of the material.

Lean in, you say.

And so I press on, into the unknowing.

Is it true that when I step through the holy door,
angels await to take the measure of my heart?

My life's worth hinges on vignettes of love, the selfless kind.

It's the secret, isn't it?

A sacrificial heart.

The more I love, the more my flesh illumines its divinity.

I pray for more breaths, more grains of sand in the hourglass

To live this one life well.

Today is a new day; may I rise to the occasion.

Walking always in the direction of love.

Amen.

YOU ARE—WE ALL ARE—THE BELOVED
OF THE BELOVED.
AND IN EVERY MOMENT, IN EVERY EVENT
OF YOUR LIFE,
THE BELOVED IS WHISPERING EXACTLY WHAT YOU
NEED TO HEAR AND KNOW.

RUMI

he Angel speaks:

Does your heart have an imagination?

The miracle play is about to commence.

Take your place.

You have been cast to play: your one true self.

The soul always gets the lead.

Leave it to humanity to fumble in the darkness backstage
when salvation is within grasp.

Peek beyond the curtain.

Don't look so surprised.

Divine Providence is seated front and center.

God always gets the best seat in the house.

Your only stage direction: Believe.

It is the one great courageous act.

The monumental questions of life threaten stage fright:

*Does my life have a special purpose? Is there a heaven?
Does the Omega really know me by name? Will there be an
end to the suffering? Why doesn't God defeat the darkness
once and for all? Will there ever be peace on earth?
Can Love really save?*

God pipes up from the balcony: Trust me.

No more posturing.

Pick up your shepherd's crook, straighten your wings,
don't forget the frankincense.

A birth is promised.

The lights come up—give in to the mystery.

Amen.

I HAVE BEEN DRIVEN MANY TIMES UPON MY KNEES
BY THE OVERWHELMING CONVICTION THAT I HAD
NOWHERE ELSE TO GO. MY OWN WISDOM AND
THAT OF ALL ABOUT ME SEEMED INSUFFICIENT
FOR THAT DAY.

ABRAHAM LINCOLN

oly One,

Disappointment is inevitable, unavoidable and
the price of being human.

It shakes the grounding of my being.

Parent, child, spouse, friend, work colleague, the person
sitting one pew ahead in church, even the curious stranger
has the power to distort my view.

And one is assured the craving body will betray as well.

Disappointment punctures a hole in the Whole.

I weep in secret, calling into question the greater Design.

If I'm not careful, this heart will callous—

My nom de plume transcribed "the Cynic."

At the crossroads of every disappointment, there are two directions
I may take: the way of the mausoleum of despair,

Or turn the corner heavenward.

Kneeling at the altar, Divine consolation at hand,
I choose to rise for another day.

Hope does not disappoint.

Amen.

AND YOU SHALL LOVE THE LORD YOUR GOD
WITH ALL YOUR HEART, AND WITH ALL YOUR
SOUL, AND WITH ALL YOUR MIGHT.

DEUTERONOMY 6:5

y God,

Please enter in where You already abide.

Although my life is measured in breaths,
You only take notice of my heart.

It makes little difference whether I am wet behind the ears,
my faith as green as the young stallion in the corral, or like
the mystic, radiating wisdom from her third eye.

Every day is an experiment in love.

Haunted by the presence of evil and frightened by its
unpredictability, I sometimes underestimate the power of love.

Stubborn as a mule, I grab the reins, convinced I can
control how this planet turns,

When all You ever asked of me was to trust.

Remember, You said,

I will not leave you until I have done what I have promised.

Wake me up before it is too late.

I want to live my life, every single breath, in the hope of all that is,
all that is promised and all that will be.

May I never forget that I bear the soul of God within me.

Amen.

WHATEVER HAPPENS,
THOSE WHO HAVE LEARNED
TO LOVE ONE ANOTHER
HAVE MADE THEIR WAY
TO THE LASTING WORLD
AND WILL NOT LEAVE,
WHATEVER HAPPENS.

WENDELL BERRY

 od,

Thank You for being my steadfast and true.

The one who knows the exact curve of my smile, the count of
every freckle, and the canticle of my heart, holy and not.

The one who weeps when I fall, brushes the salt from my cheek,
wipes my slate clean, a jubilee, and helps me to rise for another day.

The one who chooses to see the best in me even when
I cannot see it for myself.

The one who doesn't flinch when I whisper my darkest secrets,
unspoken fears and breath-heavy doubts.

The one who loves me when no one else in his or
her right mind should.

After all these years, all the times I have let You down, chosen
others over You, doubted Your powers, even Your love for me,

And there You are, still, by my side—

My steadfast and true.

A friendship of divine proportions.

I am so unworthy.

And yet love bears all.

Even me.

A grateful amen.

THERE IS ONLY ONE WORLD AND THAT IS THE
SUPERNATURAL ONE.

PIERRE TEILHARD DE CHARDIN

oly One,

I come before You this day, my mind and heart aflutter.

Will this be the moment I leap forward into the mystical unknown?

Will my life reflect a glimmer of the Transcendent?

Or has my story become so neat, orderly, predictable,

Earthly–

That my spirit has become calloused to the miracle?

Life's path is uncertain and often comes with a heavy load:

Ailing bodies, weeping spirits, broken relationships
and fragile faiths.

And yet my soul still retains the
unmistakable silhouette of the Divine.

I am desperate to feel something far greater
than this world can provide:

Angels, supernovas and resurrections!

I am made of stardust.

See me shine.

Amen.

BE HUMBLE FOR YOU ARE MADE OF DUNG.
BE NOBLE FOR YOU ARE MADE OF STARS.

SERBIAN PROVERB

eloved,

How do I begin to say thank You?

In my humble garb of flesh and bone,
I whisper thank You for all that I am—

Divinely made, tenderly loved and eternally bound.

How do I say thank You for all that You give?

For that first holy breath and every one of them since, where You
continue to breathe love and hope and grace into my very marrow.

How do I say thank You for the exquisite beauty of my soul—

That one part of me that the world cannot have

Because it belongs to You.

The place where You dwell so I am never alone.

The place that radiates Your glory and is charged with delivering
Your message of love into creation.

How do I say thank You for giving me my mother and my father,
sisters and brothers, sons and daughters, friends and foes,
neighbors and strangers—

To practice love, to practice healing, to practice mercy,
to practice grace on Your behalf?

How do I say thank You for the obstacles placed in my path—the
bruised knees and broken hearts—that reveal how strong and
resilient You created me to be?

How do I say thank You for the second, third and infinite chances
You offer me to try again and again to live a life that honors You?

Ho do I say thank You, dear Beloved?

I say thank You—

When I give You my heart.

Amen.

WITHOUT GOING OUT MY DOOR, I CAN KNOW ALL
THINGS ON EARTH.
WITHOUT LOOKING OUT MY WINDOW,
I CAN KNOW THE WAYS OF HEAVEN.

TAO TE CHING

lmighty,

When did I allow the metronome of the material world
to become my favored timepiece?

I fear my soul has fallen off rhythm.

Where is the holiness in the busyness?

I put my fingers to my ears, anything to hear again
Your still, small voice beneath the babel.

You know my heart.

Unleash the mystic, the buddha, the Christ living inside of me.

I must reclaim my divinity if I am to be of any use to You.

Send me an Ebenezer so that I would remember again who I am—

Who You believe I can be.

Test the grounding of my being so that I might give
account of the hope that lives inside of me.

It is time I step outside of myself so that others may see
Your glow in my face.

With the hem of my spirit threaded in mercy,
today I will be love for You.

A sincere amen.

THE GLORY OF GOD IS A HUMAN BEING
FULLY ALIVE.

St. Irenaeus

earest God,

You slipped Your spirit into the livery of flesh and bone,
then walked this planet for a time, keeping it secret that
You were the prince of the heavens.

Sent on a divine mission, Your purpose was to show me
how I am to live in this world.

With dusty, sandaled feet, a humble countenance, heart in
Your hands and a disposition of hope,

You tried Your best to show me the way.

How was I to know I was in such need of saving?

You grieve at how easily I can lose my way.

One moment I am two steps behind You, the next, utterly lost.

My ego overshadows my intuitive heart.

I am in a tug of war of loyalties.

There is the world that seduces, tells me that power, status and
material wealth are the secrets to the crown.

And then there is Your voice whispering deep within me,
commanding me to serve, speak a dialect of love, see the unseen,
and lift up the lost and forgotten.

It's time I start focusing on heaven's scorecard
instead of the world's.

Thank You for still believing I have something worthy
to offer this world in Your Holy Name.

Amen.

Turn the spotlight inward.

Mahatma Gandhi

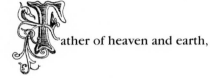ather of heaven and earth,

In You I move, breathe and have my being.

You have graciously anointed me with
an angel's mission here on earth.

Remind me again how to reach down into my divine depths and
rise up to take my hallowed place in the love story.

Forgive me when I allow the evils of this world to send me off
course, lean into this world instead of stargaze for my direction
and underestimate that love is more than enough
to accomplish the business of heaven.

I pray for another day to be illumined by Your spirit, so that I might
do something to make You proud to call me Your own.

My heart belongs to You.

Amen.

TRUTH IS FOUND BY LIVING TRULY.

Lama Surya Das

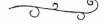

y God,

I come before You today looking for answers to
the questions of my heart.

How do I know if I am living the life You dreamed for me?

How many dead ends and broken hearts must I endure
before I wake up and find You at my center?

What is the substance of holy things?

I know it is not power, a royal title, glory, wealth or beauty.

These turn to dust right before my eyes.

Please open my heart and lay the truth there.

Everything but You is unpredictable, fragile, flawed
and many times heartbreaking.

I raise my hands up to You, crying out the world has come undone.

I yearn to burrow in safe underneath Your everlasting wings.

Tell me You will make things right.

Promise me that love will prevail in the end.

Give me the courage to stake my whole being in Your holy court.

The truth was always there for me: Love.

Love You with my whole heart, mind, strength and soul,
and then love my neighbor as myself.

It is the secret to my salvation.

Amen.

GOD BENEATH YOU.
GOD IN FRONT OF YOU.
GOD BEHIND YOU.
GOD ABOVE YOU.
GOD WITHIN YOU.

ST. PATRICK'S BREASTPLATE PRAYER

od,

When I call out to You, "My Father," the distance between
the heavens and my heart suddenly disappears.

And there I am standing in the presence of love.

You know me so intimately: every scar, glaring flaw, the count of
my tears, my secret dreams and especially my need for You.

How is it that You disregard the chinks in my armor?

The places in my life where I have hurt those I love, disappointed
myself, but more importantly, disavowed You.

And yet steadfast You continue to see the potential of my heart.

Days, weeks, months can go by with no word, and then I trumpet the
heavens in desperation, with a litany of requests upon my tongue.

And there You are as promised.

You open Your arms, pull me into You, and all seems possible again.

No wrath, no judgment, only compassion.

Patiently, You listen from Your throne in the stars as I whisper my
fears, count my losses and beg pardon for my faults.

What would I do, what would become of me, if I could not call out
"My Father" and know that You would be there for me as close as my
breath and as near as my heartbeat?

That is where You dare, ready to take my hand and walk me through
the shadows into the light again.

How will I ever be able to respond to the gravity
of this kind of love?

I cannot.

But I will spend my remaining breaths trying.

A humble amen.

KEEP SOME ROOM IN YOUR HEART
FOR THE UNIMAGINABLE.

MARY OLIVER

he One and true,

You are my lifeline—

The one absolute that I can hold steadfast
in the exquisite and the tragic.

In that holy moment when You breathed life into my dust,
You activated Your living spirit deep within me.

You made me Your vessel of honor, then set me free
to discover my unique destiny.

It was and always will be about love for You.

How far, wide and deep am I willing to go
and be stretched in the name of that love?

I have no idea the power You entrusted at the throne of my heart.

If there was ever a time when You needed me to rise up and do
something exceptional in Your name—

The time is now.

Help me do Your will in this conflicted world.

May my soul tell a story of love.

Amen.

WHEN THE EYES OF THE SOUL LOOKING OUT
MEET THE EYES OF GOD LOOKING IN,
HEAVEN HAS BEGUN RIGHT HERE ON EARTH.

A.W. TOZER

oliest One,

Are You listening?

Can You hear the silent whisperings of my heart?

I fear I have lost my way.

The earth journey is full of adventure and great challenges, light
and darkness, niggling doubts and surprising revelations of hope.

I am foolish to think I can travel the path on my own accord.

Forgive my breath of hubris.

I need You, Divine One, to be my inner compass when there are no
stars in my sky, to be my touchstone when the world disappoints
and to be my hope when my spirit leans toward doubt.

Inspire the priest, the healer, the angel, the prophet,
the lowly one in me.

Make me into Your hero.

And I will be Your light. I will be Your hope. I will be Your
forgiveness. I will be Your mercy.

I will be Your love.

There is so much work to be done, so many hearts to save.

Together, let us begin.

Amen.

I am He whom I love,
and He whom I love is I.

Mansur Al-Hallaj

eloved,

It is a miracle.

The more I love, the more Your holy and
mysterious story makes sense.

The more I love, the closer I become to who You created me to be.

The more I love, the better I see You in all and everything.

Today is a new day in the cosmic mission of love.

I shall transcend this flesh and bone, pay heed to the intuition of
my soul and gather my courage to give my heart away.

Every time I do this, a little piece of me is redeemed.

And I move one step closer to Your kingdom.

Amen.

WHY ARE YOU SO ENCHANTED BY THIS WORLD
WHEN A MINE OF GOLD LIES WITHIN YOU?

RUMI

ivine One,

You are not afraid of my flaws and imperfections

But instead embrace them.

Tenderly, You mend my broken places with gold dust,

Transforming me into something more luminous than before.

It is in the breaks and shattering that You see my value.

Resilient.

I am more beautiful for having been broken.

I bear a gilded heart.

Next time the porcelain suffers a crack, may I not be so afraid.

The Master Potter works in gold.

Amen.

THE MOST IMPORTANT, THE MOST REAL
AND LASTING WORK OF THE CHRISTIAN IS
ACCOMPLISHED IN THE DEPTHS OF HIS OWN SOUL.
IT CANNOT BE SEEN BY ANYONE, EVEN BY HIMSELF.
IT IS KNOWN ONLY TO GOD.

THOMAS MERTON

oving God,

I suffer from a secret gnawing, soul deep, that nothing
of this world can satisfy.

What I yearn for is to experience an encounter with Your divine
mystery—a peek through the veil.

You say, "Look inside."

I forget that the coordinates of heaven are etched across my heart.

From my beginning, even in the womb, You laid a bread crumb trail
of hope for me to follow, confident that one day
I would find my way back to You.

Forgive me when I lose my way, stumble
and succumb to a devil's dead end.

When life's path falls into darkness,
lay markers of hope to light my way.

When life wrestles me down like a thief in the night,
send Your fleet of angels in rescue.

When my weary spirit cannot take another step, nourish my soul
on morsels of Your grace so that I may continue on.

Heaven is within my reach.

Take me by the hand and I will follow.

Amen.

CHRIST COULD BE BORN A THOUSAND TIMES
IN BETHLEHEM—BUT ALL IN VAIN UNTIL HE
IS BORN IN ME.

ANGELUS SILESIUS

 nfinite One,

The Angel Gabriel has spoken.

The Mother of God has sung her Magnificat in reply.

The star of hope is stitched upon the dark canvas, a luminous
protagonist in the duel with the night.

The host of the heavenly wait for their cue,
Alleluias wet upon their gilt tongues.

The shepherds stargaze, honored to be invited into heaven's secret.

The Wise Men brave the uncertain road of life,
a mustard seed of faith ripening in their breasts.

Pay attention, Herod is cunning.

The innkeeper claims no room in the inn.

But the human heart is already dilated, the miracle is crowning.

The whole world holds its breath for a babe's mewl.

God dons the mantle of flesh well,

But there is a holier purpose:

The remedy of humanity.

Love is the crux.

Tell the story again.

This time, my soul wishes a part to play.

Amen.

REMEMBER, I AM WITH YOU.
I WILL NOT LEAVE YOU UNTIL I HAVE DONE WHAT
I PROMISED.

GENESIS 28:15

oly and loving God,

You say You are not distant, enthroned in the heavens;

You are standing right here in front of me.

You are the child who refuses to stop smiling despite
the gnawing hunger in her belly.

You are today's Job, who's lost everything but keeps
looking to the heavens for salvation.

You are the woman perfumed in stale liquor spewing curses from
the street corner, desperate to know unconditional love.

You are the lost teen, the weeping widow, the blind man, the
adulterer and the cancer patient.

You say You are living inside my very own fragile heart.

Entangled in my own life and needs, overwhelmed by the gravity
and unpredictability of this world, I often miss You.

You say You are my way, my truth and my life. You will travel
to the ends of the world for me, for the child, for the widow,
for the sinner and the saint.

Can I dare to believe?

My life depends on it.

Amen.

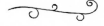

LORD JESUS CHRIST, SON OF GOD,
HAVE MERCY ON ME, A SINNER.

PRAYER OF THE HEART

y God,

What a scary reality if You forgave me how I often forgive others—

Blame, shame, guilt, resentment, even revenge.

But that's not love and that's not who You are.

You look past the ugly and see the potential of
something beautiful and redeemable.

You never lose hope in the inherent goodness of the human heart.

You know that underneath my skin, the DNA is divine. And so when I break
Your heart, tripping over my own humanity, Your response is mercy. You
believe I deserve a second chance.

God, as much as I embrace forgiveness as a lovely idea, when I actually have
to live it, I fall short.

I hold on to my hurts until they define me. I allow my heart to become
calloused in the name of self-preservation.

I think that by denying forgiveness I gain power,
when in reality, it diminishes all that I am.

All the while, the distance between You and me
just grows wider and wider.

There can be another way. It's called mercy. But it requires a great deal of
courage, vulnerability, and a leap into holy contradiction. It actually means
that I must present my heart to the one who broke it in the first place.

But when I choose mercy, suddenly I find myself in a state of grace.

For the first time, I experience a tiny ripple of Your holy power.

I am set free.

Free to heal. Free to hope again. Free to dream of tomorrow.
Free to love and be loved.

Help me to remember that forgiveness is lightning in a bottle.

Once it's released — Nothing by the grace of God —
can ever be the same.

Amen.

THE PRAYER PRECEDING ALL PRAYERS IS
"MAY IT BE THE REAL I WHO SPEAKS.
MAY IT BE THE REAL THOU THAT I SPEAK TO."

C.S. LEWIS

 od,

Today I step into the Confessional of my soul.

Here in the quiet, it's just You, me and the truth.

What a frightening reality, because I cannot hide anything from You.

Every flaw in the diamond is exposed to Your scrutiny.

How small my life must sometimes appear to You.

Can You forgive me when I have allowed fear to shrink me to
cowardice, paid heed to the world instead of Your still, small voice
inside me, held back forgiveness, thought only of myself
and shamefully taken Your love for granted?

You designed a miracle when You designed my heart.

In the small and ordinary, and with the littlest gestures of sacrifice,
acts of kindness and displays of mercy, I am redeemed.

You offer me the chance to return into Your holy favor.

My heart absolved.

One day I hope to be finally counted on the side of
Your grace eternally.

Amen.

SOMETHING IS VERY GENTLY,
INVISIBLY, SILENTLY,
PULLING AT ME — A THREAD
OR NET OF THREADS
FINER THAN COBWEB AND AS
ELASTIC.
...WAS I
BORN WITH ITS KNOT ABOUT MY
NECK, A BRIDLE? NOT FEAR
BUT A STIRRING
OF WONDER MAKES ME
CATCH MY BREATH WHEN I FEEL
THE TUG OF IT WHEN I THOUGHT
IT HAD LOOSENED ITSELF AND GONE.

DENISE LEVERTOV

ather,

I do not come before You with flowery and ornate words,
only a humble plea to allow Your transcendent
presence to enfold all that I am.

It is so difficult not knowing what lies ahead.

I need something larger than myself
and this world to tether my heart.

Are You who I am looking for?

Will You remain steadfast in the intimate details of my life, fierce in
handling my fears, my doubts and disappointments, but also tender
enough to collect my tears and hold me through the night?

Pull now on that invisible thread that connects
the center of my being to You.

Then I can float in the hope, knowing that I am not alone.

You have me.

And my story will continue on.

Amen.

FAITH IS THE RADICAL TRUST THAT HOME HAS
ALWAYS BEEN THERE AND ALWAYS WILL BE THERE.

HENRI NOUWEN

lmighty One,

I live in this mysterious space in between—

In the world and yet not completely of the world,
clothed in the fragility of flesh and bone, and yet
mysteriously inhabited by a lighted soul.

Thank You for including me in Your luminous experiment of love.

You never promised it would be easy.

To love is to suffer.

And thus, I live in a world full of broken hearts.

But what You do promise is that if I hold fast to what is good,
be patient in my suffering, persevere in my prayers,
turn the other cheek and give more than I take,
You will prove to me that love will bear all.

More importantly, that love will save me.

Help me now to live by, in and for the Spirit, trusting in the
promise of all that I am—flesh, bone and soul—
to further Your mission of love.

Amen.

YOUR ENTIRE LIFE IS YOUR PRAYER.

DR. NORMAN VINCENT PEALE

oving God,

You have chosen me to play a special role
in the history of the world.

I walk the path set before me, placing one foot in front of the other,
trying my best to make my way with some measure of grace.

It requires courage to live in this frenetic material world without
surrendering that most pure and beautiful part of me.

Remove the scales from my eyes, send Your angels to strike my
Achilles' heel of pride, dose me with Your glory.

Remind me that I was not created for my own pleasure
but for the service of love.

And I will rise up and realize Your dreams for me.

I will mend that which is broken, lift up those who have fallen,
feed the hungry with tender morsels of love, touch the wounded in
body and spirit, pray and pray some more.

Only then will I help bring the heavens to earth.

When Your angels open up the holy door to welcome me home, I
pray I have left worthy footprints in the dust.

Amen.

SHUT YOUR EYES, SHUT YOUR MOUTH
AND OPEN YOUR HEART.

St. John Vianney

aster architect of love,

I am calling out to You today from that most intimate and secret place of my being, yearning to touch the hem of Your robe and feel Your mysterious power ripple through me.

You see my broken seams, the rips and tears where I have been hurt, the keen losses, the cruel disappointments, the ugly mistakes due to pride and my paralyzing fears of the unknown.

This business of being human is not for the faint of heart.

I am the fragile woman at the well in need of Your healing waters, stubborn Paul on the road to Damascus ripe for a conversion, and doubting Thomas desperate to touch the supernatural to believe.

My heart desires for more, a larger stake in Your glory plan, a chance to do something really beautiful with my life in Your name.

You ask, *How big is your brave?*

It is time I show You.

First, I must acknowledge with gratitude Your faithful presence in my life.

Second, I must honor You by determining Your will for my life, then use every remaining breath to try and fulfill it.

And finally, I must walk this planet in reverence for even the chance to participate in the smallest way and for however long in Your love story.

Amen.

I KNOW MYSELF BECAUSE YOU, GOD, KNOW ME.

THOM SCHUYLER

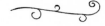

oly One,

The moment You breathed life into me and tenderly tucked
Your divine light deep within my soul—

You made me a promise.

Nothing.

Not this life, not my darkest night, not even my death
will ever keep us apart.

Why do I have such a difficult time believing in this beautiful truth?

I look to my left and to my right.

I become impatient.

I doubt.

I pound my chest and curse the heavens.

I turn my back on You.

You remain steadfast by my side,
ready to tuck me in closer under Your wings.

In that still, small voice, You whisper,
I see you. I hear you. I hold you.

This is love.

It makes me brave, resilient, hopeful and full of faith.

It makes me believe.

Amen.

Hover over me, God

St. Teresa d'Avila

rince of Peace,

My breaths take place somewhere between the darkness
and the light, my material desires and spiritual needs,
my doubts and my faith in You.

I tug on the sacred rope that connects me to You—

Only to have the earthly world pull me right back.

There are too many unknowns and grave disparities between
heaven and earth for my mind and heart to reconcile.

The heaviness and unpredictability pin my heart inside my chest.

If only I could breathe free.

Knowing in my deep that whatever I must face, You have me.

At the end of my rope,

There You will always be.

Amen.

YOU HAVE MADE US FOR YOURSELF, AND OUR
HEART IS RESTLESS UNTIL IT RESTS IN YOU.

ST. AUGUSTINE

eloved,

What is the secret to entering Your kingdom?

The world would have me believe it physical beauty, the
distinguished job, health, wealth and personal security.

How naive.

The more I accumulate, rely on my own powers,
try and control my present and my tomorrow,

The poorer, the emptier, the more lost I feel—

The further I am from Your kingdom.

All the riches of this world will eventually turn to dust.

Even my flesh and bone will fade away.

The secret to entering Your kingdom is through my selfless heart.

Today I will give a piece of mine away.

Amen.

IF WE TRULY WANT TO FOLLOW GOD,
WE MUST SEEK TO BE OTHERWORLDLY.

A.W. TOZER

ivine One,

By whose love all things come into being,

You have blessed me with a world thick with divine possibility.

Tucked in the satchel of my heart lives a fleck of Your glory.

It is a mighty responsibility.

With immense humility, I will try and touch the hurt of this world,
speak words of hope into the dark void and rise up tall against the
giants of injustice, seeing not race nor color nor sex nor religion.

Only the dignity of every soul.

Anoint me again as Your holy creature.

May my life be a living testament—

Love is the point.

Amen.

PARADISE IS AT YOUR OWN CENTER.
UNLESS YOU FIND IT THERE, THERE IS
NO WAY TO ENTER.

ANGELUS SILESIUS

erciful God,

I am Your sacred pilgrim on the road of life,
bearing with me a compass of flickering faith.

It is a real test not knowing what to expect around the next bend.

There are moments that I nearly float, life the picture of bliss.

Other times I feel as if I'm walking in dark circles,

Or, worse, stopped in place.

I throw my hands up in the air—

Confused and frightened, even angry at the path You have set
before me.

I question You.

Why the evil, the pain, the suffering, the loss, the uncertainty?

It chokes my spirit.

And then there is death, the unavoidable,
razor-sharp truth that cuts to the quick of every soul.

True faith is having the courage to walk whatever path is set before
me and practice patience when the things of this world make little
sense and prove cruelly unfair.

Faith is a day-to-day muscling through—

Because You promise I will make it to the other side.

Faith is the heart's certainty:

One day the path will lead me back eternally to You.

Amen.

WHITHERSOEVER YOU TURN,
THERE IS THE FACE OF GOD.

QURAN 2:115

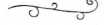

od,

You engraved Your love upon my soul so that I would know in the
depths of my being to whom I belong.

Could there be anything more wondrous?

You, the Almighty One, invested in lowly me.

You never doubt that one day I will rise up and manifest Your holy
dreams for me.

Forgive me for letting You down.

I say I love You,

And yet often my life does not reflect this truth.

I can and must do better for You if I have any chance
of honoring the gift that is my life.

Help me to be less afraid of what I cannot see
and instead more daring with my heart.

Encourage my inner curiosity of matters of the spirit so that I begin
to see the larger picture and my place in it.

Take my hand and lead me where I was always meant to go.

It is my heart's dream.

Amen.

LOVE GUARDS THE HEART FROM THE ABYSS.

WOLFGANG AMADEUS MOZART

oly and loving God,

When will I learn?

How many times must I turn away from You?

Cut corners in my faith, hedge my bets,
try to worship both You and the world.

Fail miserably.

Feel alone.

Only to have You chase after me,

Mercy in one hand, grace in the other,

Gifting me with another chance.

You whisper, *I love you. You belong to me.*

Do I have any idea what that means?

It means I belong to You—

The one who will go the distance to save me
from myself and from this broken world.

The one who is not afraid to enter the darkness, face my demons,
forgive my grievous faults and see all as an opportunity for grace.

May I never underestimate the gravity of this kind of love.

You love me.

I belong to You.

Amen.

THEN JACOB AWOKE FROM HIS SLEEP AND SAID,
"SURELY THE LORD IS IN THIS PLACE; AND I DID
NOT KNOW IT."

GENESIS 28:16

ather in heaven,

Thank You for even the darkness, for then I am able to see Your light.

So much of my earthly life, I muddle through in the dark with no access to Your divine master plan nor opportunity to take a peek at the future chapters of my human story.

I become anxious.

Instead of trusting You to be in control of my today
and my tomorrow,

I take the reins—

Reins twisted and knotted in worry—

And try to strike out into the dark alone.

I forget that I was never meant to carry the burden
of my humanity on my own.

If only for a breath, one inhale and exhale,

I could remember just who You are—

You are my savior.

You are my God who promises I will never be left alone.

You are my God who proves that no amount of pain, uncertainty or darkness can keep Your love from entering in and redeeming.

You are my God who tenderly takes the reins from
my hands and says,

Let me have a turn.

Amen.

OUR JOURNEYS ALL START AND END WITH GOD,
AND EVERYTHING WE DO IS A STEP TOWARD OUR
RETURN TO WHOLENESS.

BECCA STEVENS

eloved,

I am in awe of Your daring plan of love for all of creation.

Just when I begin to despair, Your light rises up
and defeats life's day-to-day darkness.

When will I trust that the cobalt sky
and the gilt sun is always there?

It is only the clouds that come and go.

I have to choose to believe that You will provide me
with a new vision—holy and redemptive.

I have to choose to believe in hope.

I have to choose to believe in resurrections, small
and grand as the order of the day.

I have to choose to believe Your love will save me.

But when I do, the world can never be the same again.

Amen.

AS SWIMMERS DARE
TO LIE FACE TO THE SKY
AND WATER BEARS THEM,
AS HAWKS REST UPON AIR
AND AIR SUSTAINS THEM,
SO WOULD I LEARN TO ATTAIN
FREEFALL, AND FLOAT
INTO CREATOR SPIRIT'S DEEP EMBRACE,
KNOWING NO EFFORT EARNS
THAT ALL-SURROUNDING GRACE.

DENISE LEVERTOV

ender of Creation,

How can You stand by and watch Your creation struggle
and hurt and succumb to evil?

Why won't You stop the wars of families, countries, faiths?

Don't You hate the withering of bodies and spirits,
the loss of dignity and hope, the betrayals, the fears,
the unseen wounds and finally, death?

It surely makes You weep a tempest.

But You are writing a different story.

I need to hear *this* story.

Our world needs to hear *this* timeless story of love again and again.

It is the story of how love prevails every single time.

Mend my heart and mend my world.

Send Your angels in protection.

Speak to me from the cross a tale of miracles and resurrections.

My heart never tires of a love story,

Especially with You as the Author.

Amen.

EVEN THE DARKNESS IS NOT DARK TO YOU; THE
NIGHT AS BRIGHT AS THE DAY. FOR DARKNESS IS
LIGHT TO YOU.

PSALM 139:12

ord of Love,

Call out to me.

Call out to me from the shore and ask me to follow You.

I have spent my life fishing.

Fishing for something that would make me feel whole, healed,
important and worthy.

My net keeps coming up empty.

I am always the busy fisherman, trying my best to make sense of
this world and my place in it.

My ego, with my stubborn determination to captain my own life
ship, keeps me from hearing Your delicate call to follow You.

To put You in charge.

To trust You with my today and tomorrow.

Especially when the skies grow dark, rough seas test the strength of
my boat and I have no idea where the winds will blow me.

Call out to me.

Call out to me from the shore and ask me again to follow You.

Ask me to surrender and choose Your grace.

It's a risk.

It means I must love better, forgive even the ones who have really
hurt me, champion the dignity of my brother and touch the hurts
of the lepers of this world.

To follow You means I cannot judge, only embrace.

It means I have to trust You that even when nothing makes sense
all around me, and this life brings me to my knees, You will be there
as promised to lead me to another shore.

May this be the day that I hear You call to my heart—

And I follow.

Amen.

GOD SPEAKS TO EACH OF US AS HE MAKES US,
THEN WALKS WITH US SILENTLY OUT OF THE
NIGHT.
THESE ARE THE WORDS WE DIMLY HEAR:
YOU, SENT OUT BEYOND YOUR RECALL,
GO TO THE LIMITS OF YOUR LONGING.
EMBODY ME.
FLARE UP LIKE FLAME
AND MAKE BIG SHADOWS I CAN MOVE IN.
LET EVERYTHING HAPPEN TO YOU: BEAUTY AND
TERROR.
JUST KEEP GOING. NO FEELING IS FINAL.
DON'T LET YOURSELF LOSE ME.
NEARBY IS THE COUNTRY THEY CALL LIFE.
YOU WILL KNOW IT BY ITS SERIOUSNESS.
GIVE ME YOUR HAND.

MARIA RAINER RILKE

rchitect of love,

My soul is calling out to You.

There are broken seams in my tapestry in need of Your care, dark corners desperate for illumination, and places of deep and grave silence in need of a word of hope.

See how I wrestle with my humanity.

And yet Your spark faithfully resides deep within me.

I know it when I dare to dream of a world where the light defeats the darkness every time, where love bears all things and real hope never disappoints.

It is a dream where death is just a blink of the eye and heaven is my divine inheritance.

But that is Your master plan of love, isn't it?

It's time I stop living on the edges of Your grace and live Your dream from my holy center.

Amen.

THE FEATHER FLEW,
NOT BECAUSE OF ANYTHING IN ITSELF BUT
BECAUSE THE AIR BORE IT ALONG.
THUS AM I, A FEATHER ON THE BREATH OF GOD.

ST. HILDEGARD OF BINGEN

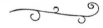

rince of Peace,

In You I live and breathe.

Your Holy Spirit percolates in my marrow,
lighting me from the inside out.

I am Your beloved, wonderfully and fearfully made,
and destined to be cherished for all time.

Today I will seek to discover what that means,

This unfathomable gift—

To carry the soul of God within me.

I recognize that my life is not my own but Yours,
to serve a higher purpose.

I have been entrusted with a mission of love.

Forgive me when I allow the evils of the world to haunt me,
underestimate the power of love to sustain me
and let my frailties define me.

All You ever asked of me was to trust.

And whisper, whenever and however and to whomever,
that love is all and enough.

Open up the holy door,

Send forth a wind from the heavens today,
a gust so strong that my soul stands at attention,

And You come alive within me.

Amen.

FEAR NOT, FOR I AM WITH YOU,
BE NOT DISMAYED, FOR I AM YOUR GOD;
I WILL STRENGTHEN YOU, I WILL HELP YOU,
I WILL UPHOLD YOU WITH MY VICTORIOUS
RIGHT HAND.

ISAIAH 41:10

oly and merciful Father,

Today, tomorrow, every day of my life, I need to hear You say,

I am with you always.

You never promised the journey would be easy.

You knew that one day I would be like David standing before a Goliath in my life.

Or Daniel in the fiery furnace, exiled from all I know to be true, desperate to find my way back home—back to You.

You knew that a day would come when, like Mary and Martha, I would rebuke You for not saving someone I loved, my heart caught in the cutting net of despair.

You knew there would be shadow days when I would struggle to see the light, days when I would walk in the valley of sorrows, days on my knees in the Garden of Gethsemane begging You to remove the cup before me.

Today, tomorrow, every day of my life, I need to hear You say,

I am with you always.

Say You are my mighty God, the God who will travel to the ends of the earth for me, the tender God who collects every tear until the joy returns in the morning, the God who carefully takes me down from the cross and resurrects my spirit, so I have life again.

Today, tomorrow, every day of my life, I need to hear You say,

I am with you always.

And I will believe.

Amen.

LISTEN TO YOUR LIFE. SEE IT FOR THE
FATHOMLESS MYSTERY THAT IT IS. IN THE
BOREDOM AND PAIN OF IT, NO LESS THAN IN
THE EXCITEMENT AND GLADNESS: TOUCH, TASTE,
SMELL YOUR WAY TO THE HOLY AND HIDDEN
HEART OF IT, BECAUSE IN THE LAST ANALYSIS,
ALL MOMENTS ARE KEY MOMENTS, AND LIFE
ITSELF IS GRACE.

FREDERICK BUECHNER

od of grace,

As I stand on the precipice of a new day, take my hand
and lead me forward into the great unknown.

I have no crystal ball, tarot card or palm reader to predict or
prepare me for what lies ahead.

Only my fragile faith in You.

Give me courage to wear nobly Your holy vestments
of flesh and bone.

Anoint my journey, the deep valleys and the mountaintops.

Unleash Your Holy Spirit to tunnel through the earthbound edges of
my being until You reach the part of me that sparkles,

The part of me that is eternal.

Thank You for the destiny You have dreamed for me.

Eyes heavenward, I will be noble in my actions, speak a patois of
love and reveal my bravery when this life grabs me by the heel.

Today I will dare to make You smile.

Amen.

BLESSED ARE THE PURE IN HEART,
FOR THEY SHALL SEE GOD.

MATTHEW 5:8

ear God,

You preached the Sermon on the Mount so that I would know how You wish me to live and be in Your world.

You asked me to follow the straight and narrow path.

You never promised it would be easy.

The glory path is a daily examen of my heart.

I confess I struggle to live day by day Your love gospel.

Sometimes this life feels too big for Your sermon to cover.

Forgive me when I allow the world's suffering, the fighting and the injustices, the battles with the body and spirit's health, broken relationships with family and friends, the curses of my ego, my pride and wavering of faith

To overwhelm, overshadow or blind me to the higher and greater purpose:

Your living and breathing homily of love.

Today is a new day.

I will take the lead of my heart.

Amen.

LORD, YOU HAVE SEARCHED ME AND KNOWN ME.
YOU KNOW WHEN I SIT DOWN AND WHEN I RISE
UP; YOU DISCERN MY THOUGHTS FROM FAR AWAY.
YOU SEARCH OUT MY PATH AND MY LYING DOWN,
AND ARE ACQUAINTED WITH ALL OF MY WAYS.
EVEN BEFORE A WORD IS ON MY TONGUE, YOU
KNOW IT COMPLETELY. YOU HEM ME IN, BEHIND
AND BEFORE, AND LAY YOUR HAND UPON ME.
SUCH KNOWLEDGE IS TOO WONDERFUL FOR ME;
IT IS SO HIGH, THAT I CANNOT ATTAIN IT.

PSALM 139:1-6

oving God,

It is a great honor to be included in Your holy story,

To know that I was created with a special part to play—

And that my life has divine importance.

With threads of lighted grace,

You weave me into the Whole.

You promise that there will not be a step, a breath, an experience
for which You will not be intimately present.

You ask so little of me—

And yet I so often take Your presence for granted.

How many times have I missed the opportunity
to know You better?

Tether my soul more intimately to You.

I will learn every divine wrinkle upon Your face.

Recognize Your tender voice above all voices.

Live a life worthy of Your love.

A life with heavenly implications.

Amen.

INTO THY HAND I COMMIT MY SPIRIT.

PSALM 31:5

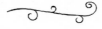

erciful Father,

It is in the dark nights of my soul, those twitching twilight hours of paralyzing fear about the unpredictability of this life, the angst about the safety and health of my family and world, and deep anxiety about death and what comes next that I struggle to remember to whom I belong and in whom I must entrust my life.

Where is my faith?

Rush in, scatter Your stardust and anoint my soul
with your grace overflowing.

Day by day I am in need of Your saving.

I hear Your invitation to breathe healing and holiness
into the vessel of my humanity.

And yet I still choose to be in control of my own destiny.

When will I learn there is no one as invested in my heart as You?

The secret to my soul's salvation is surrender.

I'm yours.

Amen.

THE HIGHEST LEVEL OF PRAYER IS NOT A PRAYER
FOR ANYTHING. IT IS A DEEP AND PROFOUND
SILENCE, IN WHICH WE ALLOW OURSELVES
TO BE STILL AND KNOW HIM.
IN THAT SILENCE, WE ARE CHANGED.

MARIANNE WILLIAMSON

Almighty God,

The road of life is set before me.

I am only permitted so many breaths in
Your gorgeous order of creation.

Between the inhales and exhales,

I experience all that it means to be human.

When life proves exquisite, my soul flushes rose within me.

But then there are the shadow days,

When heartbreak eclipses my inner sun.

I must make peace with the whole of it.

The heart must be stretched,

To transcend.

A gracious amen.

In God I move, breathe and have my being.

Acts 17:28

eloved,

Today I am Zacchaeus.

I am calling out to You from the mighty sycamore of my life.

Will You cross the threshold of my heart today?

You see me for what I truly am—

Lost.

Longing for something in my depths,

Living a life much smaller than You dreamed for me.

I don't love well enough.

I struggle to forgive.

I serve myself before You and my neighbor.

Will You cross the threshold of my heart today?

Can You look past my smallness and see my grand potential?

Say the words, *I have big plans for you.*

And my life shall be transformed forever.

Amen.

THE ONE WHO NUMBERS THE STARS
KNOWS YOU BY NAME.

PSALM 147:4

oly One,

I could have easily been one of those sleepy shepherds
that first Christmas night,

My eyes, like theirs, focused in the fields of this world.

I fumble in the dark, trying my best to find my way
and tend to my daily responsibilities—

Oblivious to the supernatural happenings all around me.

Help me to look up and see a star,

A flicker of radiant light on a dark night,

A celestial sign to show me the way.

Just like those first shepherds, may I stumble into Your grace.

Your love for me defies all reason.

You proved that so beautifully with a babe in a manger.

You came down in the flesh to show me the truth.

It is quite a beautiful story—

Of a guiding star; of wandering, helpless shepherds; of wise men,
extraordinary and brave; of a heavenly host of angels; and of a
precious infant in a lowly manger.

But the story continues to unfold every day.

My story.

Emmanuel—God with me.

Again I say: Emmanuel.

Amen.

I believe; help my unbelief!

Mark 9:24

ivine One,

You know my heart better than I do.

I believe; help my unbelief.

If I had been a guest at the Wedding at Cana,
I fear I might have proclaimed,

"There's no wine, only water in these cisterns,"

Instead of leaning into the Mystery.

Fill this empty vessel of my soul with the rich wine
of Your Holy Spirit. Allow it to spill over into
every nook, cranny and crevice of my being.

Transform my heart into a divining rod.

Make me believe again in miracles.

I don't want to ever be surprised by Your unfathomable love for me.

In secret, my soul has always known it was wine,
not water, in those cisterns.

Amen.

THAT PRAYER IS MOST PURE IN WHICH THE MONK
IS NO LONGER AWARE OF HIMSELF OR OF THE FACT
THAT HE IS PRAYING.

St. Anthony of the Desert

ather in heaven,

Thank You for the blessing of whispered prayers
when I have nowhere else to turn.

Thank You for the promise that there is no place, no time, no
amount of sorrow or joy into which You cannot enter.

Thank You for loving me in all of my beauty and imperfections.

Thank You for tucking deep within me Your Holy Spirit, ensuring I
would always have a glow, even in the depths of life's darkness.

Thank You for my heart and its supernatural capacity
to love and be loved.

Thank You for hope—

A living Hope

That allows me to put one foot in front of the other, trusting that
You have a divinely perfect plan for my life.

Amen.

PRAYER IS THE DOOR INTO THE
CASTLE OF MY SOUL.

St. Teresa d'Avila

 od,

I humbly approach Your altar today, offering You
the best version of myself.

But before I even cross the threshold into Your holy of holies,
I must confess the true condition of my heart.

You see in secret my imperfections and fragile faith.

I am not free to lay before Your altar a pure heart.

Quick to judge, stingy with forgiveness, wounding thoughtlessly
another's spirit and a dervish of doubts—

I bear no angel's wings.

I fear I often add to the darkness of this world by my own fears,
brokenness and insecurities.

If only I could live more gracefully,

Pirouette instead of stumble.

Every day is a labor of love to allow You to live fully within me.

Your son Jesus proved it was possible.

Now it is my turn.

Amen.

BE STILL AND KNOW THAT I AM GOD.
BE STILL AND KNOW THAT I AM.
BE STILL AND KNOW.
BE STILL.
BE.

RICHARD ROHR

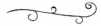

oving God,

Remind me again in Your tender, holy way that I am not alone—

That You are with me always.

I feel fragile and afraid,

Weak.

I know it is part of being human,

But it squeezes my spirit.

I cannot face another day relying on my own
limited strength and powers.

If only I could trust in the larger, mystical and
redemptive plan at work.

Give me the courage to close my eyes, bow my head
and surrender over my heart to You.

Teach me to quiet my life enough to allow You to speak a word
of clarity, hope and love into my depths.

Anoint me with Your divine understanding so I would rest assured
that whatever I must face today or tomorrow

Will not overtake me.

When the pangs of loneliness, uncertainty and fear come—
and they will—

Carry me.

In Your most tender voice, speak to my inner being:

*Be still, and know that I am your God. I have stitched you in
before and behind with my love. There is no place you can go,
even the darkest deep, that I will not be with you.*

Stardust my life with signs of Your transcendent presence—

And I will finally dare to take faith's leap.

Amen.

RETURN TO THE ROOT OF THE
ROOT OF YOUR HOLY SELF.

RUMI

eloved,

In every breath You honor me with the choice:

To love or not to love.

It proves both at once—the most simple and the
most challenging task.

I can love when I open my hands in a peace offering to the one
who disappoints me. I can love when I reach up for the tear that
spills down another's cheek. I can love when I listen to the cries of
a broken heart or stand up for a spirit wronged. I can love when I
lift my lantern in the angry spaces that hide in the darkness.

I can love in a simple word of hope.

I can love by inviting Your presence into my every conversation
with the world.

Finally, I can love when I dare to sacrifice my heart for a
cause greater than myself.

When You ask, *How well do you love for me?*

The truth: Not well enough.

May my next breath set me free from whatever is keeping me
from loving better in your holy name.

Amen.

WE ARE FULL OF PARADISE WITHOUT KNOWING IT.

THOMAS MERTON

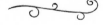

oly One,

How can I invite a little more of the mystery,
the miraculous and the transcendent into my life?

In the quiet, my soul longs for more:

More beauty, more love, more miracles.

I want to twirl through the ephemeral veil, listen for an angel's
sonata, live in a state of awe of Your glory.

Plant in me something of the heavens so that I will dream of
a bigger and more sacred life for myself.

If not, what's this all for anyway?

Amen.

WHEN WE ARE WALKING OUR CHOSEN PATH, WE
WALK ELEGANTLY, EMANATING LIGHT.

PAULO COELHO

lmighty God,

Thank You for the gift of remembering—

Remembering with every sacred stone marker planted
in the dust the saints who have come before me and
left their loving imprint on my life.

The ones who have taught me courage, to live by faith, to trust You,
to sacrifice no matter the cost for the heart of another,
and to believe in love's power to prevail.

I honor You and the saints by running the holy race set before me
with perseverance.

Who knew I had the power within me to bring the heavens to
earth with only my heart?

I will give meaning to every breath I take, loving until my heart
gives out, in the hope that one day I too could rise—

And join You and the communion of saints in eternal life.

A holiest amen.

For now we see in a mirror dimly.
Then we shall see face to face.
Now I know in part, then I shall know fully,
just as I am fully known.

1 Corinthians 13:12

rince of peace,

If only I could take a peek through Heaven's looking glass.

There is so much I do not understand here on earth.

How much energy and angst is spent in fear of the unknown, the
unpredictability and the heartbreak of this world?

I fear I miss the glimmers of Your mysterious presence working
on my behalf, always for good.

You sent me out into creation, my days numbered, with the hope
that I would use every experience to piece together the holy truth.

I may live in an imperfect world now, but You have created me with
the capacity to love perfectly.

Until I have loved to that fullest extent of my being, I will cling to
this earth and never truly see what You hoped I would see—

Love is the glorious point.

Help me to open the eyes of my heart and finally understand that
love is the answer to every question, the salve for every wound, the
direct path back to You, and the one and only truth that I can stake
my life upon now and forevermore.

Amen.

WE UNDERSTAND BY NOT UNDERSTANDING.

St. Teresa d'Avila

nfinite One,

The divine pulse of all that is and will always be for me,

You are not a secret to be kept.

And yet I often tuck You away, bury You in the business of my earthly life and turn to You only when there is nowhere else to go.

The hubris must make You tremble.

Who do I think I am?

It is only by Your grace that I get to participate in the beauty, the struggle, the heartbreak and the triumph.

All is a gift.

You are not a secret to be kept.

Let the world know my heart: You are my God and I love You.

Amen.

GOD PROVIDES MINIMUM PROTECTION,
MAXIMUM SUPPORT—SUPPORT TO HELP US GROW,
TO STRETCH OUR MINDS AND HEARTS UNTIL THEY
ARE AS WIDE AS GOD'S UNIVERSE.

WILLIAM SLOANE COFFIN

erciful Father,

You know me by my heart,

And that is a frightening truth.

It means You know who I truly am.

You know the kind of wife and husband I am. You know the kind
of mother and father I am. You know the kind of sister and brother,
friend and stranger I am.

Simply put, You know how well I love in this world.

It means very little if I am grand in stature
but walk this planet with a small heart.

To love is the greatest honor You accord to flesh and bone.

It is the secret to the glow.

The final day will come when You will ask me,
Did you love well for me?

I will not be able to hide behind the excuse of mere humanity,
for my soul will speak the truth.

There is still much "heart" work to accomplish on this side
if I am to glow eternally.

Amen.

I WANT
TO THINK AGAIN OF DANGEROUS
AND NOBLE THINGS.
I WANT TO BE LIGHT AND FROLICSOME.
I WANT TO BE IMPROBABLE BEAUTIFUL AND
AFRAID OF NOTHING,
AS THOUGH I HAD WINGS.

MARY OLIVER

ear God,

Thank You for another day to stretch my heart and evolve my soul.

Humbly, I pray for the gift of more breaths, experiences, relationships, highs and lows, tempests and rainbows—

To fully realize my potential and achieve my destiny here.

I have much still to learn about myself, about You and about how Your love makes this planet turn.

I thank You in advance for allowing me to participate in the adventure.

Amen.

WITHOUT SOLITUDE, LOVE WILL NOT STAY LONG
BY YOUR SIDE. BECAUSE LOVE NEEDS TO REST, SO
THAT IT CAN JOURNEY THROUGH THE HEAVENS
AND REVEAL ITSELF IN OTHER FORMS.

PAULO COELHO

ord of the Sabbath,

You were the first to proclaim a day of rest and mark it as holy—

Relief from a world that rewards labor, busyness, but rarely holiness.

Teach me to step away from this fragmented, frenzied and loud
earthly existence for a holy repose.

The Sabbath is a gift, permission to let go of the "work" of being
human: the stress, the fears, the doubts, the expectations, the
responsibilities, the relentless race—

And honor the needs of my soul.

It is in these moments of stillness and rest that You impart
clarity, reconcile and renew, heal, illumine and remind me
how sacred my life truly is.

I am a pearl in the palm of Your hand.

Help me to slow the spin and savor the sweet space between us.

When I step inside myself I see that not time nor the tight corset
of my humanity has a hold on me.

One day my soul will transcend and live forever.

In the meantime, I will relish its place inside me.

Amen.

LOVE BEARS ALL THINGS, BELIEVES ALL THINGS,
HOPES ALL THINGS, ENDURES ALL THINGS.

1 CORINTHIANS 13:7

od,

I find myself challenging You,
beating my chest that this life is unfair.

I have lost sight of Your mystery.

Where is Your faithful presence?

I need assurance of Your promises to see me through.

I am weak but You are strong.

Lord, carry me.

Mark me as Your own.

Set me free from whatever is keeping me from trusting my life
wholly to You and believing that Your love is enough to save me.

Take my hand and pull me back into You

And never let me go.

Amen.

WHAT LIES BEHIND US AND WHAT LIES
BEFORE US ARE TINY MATTERS COMPARED
TO WHAT LIES WITHIN US.

HENRY HASKINS

 oly One,

I say that I love you.

But am I truly *in* love with you?

Every day I waver in my devotion.

One moment I come to you with my heart in my hands, the next,
I am curled up with the world, starry-eyed with the next flashy
bauble, taking direction from my ego instead of my soul, consumed
in busyness and thinking only of myself.

I don't like how I feel when I choose the world over You.

Instead of open arms and flushed cheeks, bright eyes and words of
hope on my tongue, I become anxious, cynical and stale of joy.

It's biblical: When the salt loses its taste and the light buckles under
the weight of the darkness—all value is lost.

Take me back.

My soul is weary from looking for the next savior to fill the void
when You are standing right there in front of me.

Take me back again and again if You have to.

In my deep, I belong to You.

What greater destiny: A life spent falling in love with Love.

Amen.

HOW ELSE BUT THROUGH A BROKEN HEART
MAY LORD CHRIST ENTER IN?

Oscar Wilde

eloved,

I am afraid of the edge.

The edge of uncertainty and doubt.

The edge of my fears, heart-breaking grief and scary loneliness.

The edge of disappointment.

Disappointment in myself, in this world,
even disappointment in you, my God.

I am afraid of the edge that separates life from death
and death from life eternal.

Too close to the edge and I might lose control,
or worse, lose myself.

So I run, get quiet, or fill my life with empty distractions

Anything to protect my soul from falling.

You whisper, *Walk toward the brink, and there I will be.*

At the edge I find the face of God.

At the edge is where a divine alchemy takes place inside my soul.

At the edge is where I feel the fire stretching, evolving—Saving me.

At the edge is where a blessed transfiguration takes place.

And I become who You dreamed I could be.

Help me to be less afraid of life's edges—both the ones in front of
me and especially the ones secret within me.

At the edge, I will pray, trust, believe and hope until You see me
safely through and to the other side.

Amen.

OUR MISSION IS TO PLANT OURSELVES
AT THE GATES OF HOPE.

VICTORIA SAFFORD

lmighty God,

Sing me a heavenly melody—

A sequence of chords and notes with the power to speak over the noise of this broken world and give me hope.

When did I—Your holy creature—forget how to sing a hallelujah?

How did I allow the hurt, the darkness, the wars waged and my frightening fears to be louder than Your voice?

Have I become so jaded, self-interested and heartbroken that I no longer listen for a love song?

You and only You are the musician of my soul.

Today I will sing, "Hallelujah."

Amen.

FOR ANY SPIRIT SUDDENLY AWAKENED TO HOW
DEEP ITS LIFE, HOW SHORT ITS STAY.

MARK NEPO

oving God,

I find myself at a holy crossroads—

Who am I? To whom do I belong? Where I am going?

These questions rise up secret in me as I struggle
to live a life worthy of Your breath.

The earthly realm has proved itself quite cunning in tricking me
into believing that the keys to the kingdom are found in personal
success, self-reliance and fleeting material treasures.

And yet when the lights are turned down and I'm left standing
alone with myself, I know intimately how empty and cold this
world proves to be.

It inspires greed, jealousy, anger and fear—

Instead of true, abiding love.

This world cares little for my soul.

And yet, that is who I am.

Underneath my earthly armor, my heart is etched with the words:
Property of the Divine.

In my intimate spaces, I seek more for my existence and my time
here. I yearn for that which I can't see, store up or measure.

May I bow to You in a babe's vulnerability,

No false bravado,

And finally take the path of holiness.

A path where each stone is paved in my redemption
and seamed in Your love.

Amen.

GOD COMES TO YOU DISGUISED AS YOUR LIFE.

PAULA D'ARCY

y faithful friend,

Thank You for the gift of Your love.

It is a balm for my wounds.

A listening ear.

A giver of dignity.

A sacrificer who saves.

A bestower of joy.

A provider of security.

A fountain of compassion.

A constant encourager.

A patient forgiver.

A face that smiles.

A pair of arms to wrap around my fragile spirit.

It is this kind of supernatural love that makes me believe there is something wondrous at work here.

And I am blessed to be a part of it.

Amen.

IF THE HEART HAS HEARD THE PRAYER,
GOD HAS HEARD THE PRAYER.

LLEWELLYN VAUGHAN-LEE

ather in heaven,

You ask me to approach You with the abandon of a child.

Oh, how difficult this proves to be.

Have I walked this planet too long—

Forgotten my celestial beginnings?

When did I allow the darkness of this world to diminish
heaven's glow within me?

I fear I have allowed this world to rub away my patina of holiness.

What will it take for me to remember that I belong to You
and stand to inherit the heavens?

That no matter what happens to me here on earth, I am eternal.

I bear the unmistakable markings of Your love.

Heaven is my home.

My name is written in the stars.

Oh, to believe again with the abandon of a child.

Amen.

JUST TO BE IS A BLESSING. JUST TO LIVE IS HOLY.

RABBI ABRAHAM JOSHUA HESCHEL

ord of Love,

You continue to sit as host at the holy table of my life.

It is a table where all of me is welcome:
sinner, saint, cynic and prophet.

Some days I come to You weighted down by
the burdens of this world.

Other days I kneel flushed with joy,
so grateful for a season of blessings.

I approach You with questions about suffering,
the future and the state of my soul.

I beckon Your wisdom as to how I am to
navigate in this cynical world without losing hope.

Lord, as gracious host, You accept me wherever I am in my life.

I bow with such gratitude for even the chance
to participate in the beauty.

Continue to break the loaves and divvy out
the grace to nourish my spirit.

May I never take my seat at Your table for granted.

Amen.

BEAUTY AND GRACE ARE PERFORMED WHETHER
OR NOT WE WILL OR SENSE THEM.
THE LEAST WE CAN DO IS TRY TO BE THERE.

ANNIE DILLARD

ivine One,

With one breath You began a story here on earth for me—

Unique, blessed and full of promise.

There have been chapters that have brought me to my knees.

You have watched me stumble,
turn my back on You, curse You in the dark.

And yet here I am.

And here You are.

Together we are still writing the miracle story that is my life.

My greatest fear is not pain, nor suffering nor even death.

It is that I might not fullfill Your purpose for my life.

I want to make you proud to call me Your own.

Amen.

IN ORDER TO HEAR LOVE'S WORDS, YOU MUST
ALLOW LOVE TO APPROACH.

PAULO COELHO

od of heaven and earth,

You are my sun, my moon—A handful of stars scattered
across my darkest night.

You are the face of the great I Am.

You are that last muster of inner courage when my mind, body and
spirit want to send up the white flag of defeat.

You are the holy sacrament: the bread, the wine and the hope that
nourish the hunger of my inner being.

You are the quiet intimacy, that secret inner tug on my soul that
draws me in when the outside world proves cold and unmerciful.

You are the architect of miracles, small and grand, that prove
that nothing—not time, not suffering, not loss,
not the laws of the universe, not even death—is safe from
Your supernatural powers of grace.

You are the savior of my human heart—

The One who loves me regardless.

I humbly say amen.

GIVE ME THE COURAGE TO STAND THE PAIN TO
GET THE GRACE, OH LORD.

FLANNERY O'CONNOR

rince of peace,

You broke open the world for me that first Easter morning.

Nothing will ever be the same again.

Your love defies all.

You proved that so beautifully when You defeated death, sent Your
bevy of angels and breathed life again into Your son.

When the veil was torn in two, You revealed there was
no boundary to Your love.

No darkness, no trial, no loss, no grave that Your love could not
enter into and redeem.

How do I now live knowing this truth?

The truth that I am already saved for no other reason than because
You love me.

In the weeks following the shock-and-awe miracle of Easter, the
disciples had to make a choice:

Return to their regular lives or allow the resurrection to
dramatically reshape their hearts.

In the depths of my being, I want to be changed.

I want to live my life in such a way that You know—that I know—
what You have done for me.

A grateful amen.

AT THE CENTER OF OUR BEING IS A POINT OF
NOTHINGNESS WHICH IS UNTOUCHED BY SIN AND
BY ILLUSION, A POINT OF PURE TRUTH, A POINT
OR SPARK WHICH BELONGS ENTIRELY TO GOD.
[IT] IS THE PURE GLORY OF GOD IN US.

THOMAS MERTON

eloved,

Who am I?

Am I mere flesh clinging to now, or am I part of
a greater plan with eternal implications?

The answer lies inside.

The time has come for me to turn the spotlight inward.

I must embark on the journey in—

If I'm ever to meet my true self.

At my center, there is a mystical spark.

Who knew that I would find You there?

How can I not live in a state of wonder of all
the divine possibilities for my life?

I am beginning to like my soul.

Now I must learn how to live from my inside out.

Amen.

BE STILL, AND KNOW THAT I AM GOD.

Psalm 46:10

oliest One,

Who is a magnificent God like You?

The God whom I can call on night and day, and for as long as I live.

The God who promises to rescue me from my fears, my doubts, my brokenness in body and spirit—ultimately rescue me from death.

Who is a magnificent God like You?

The God who made me in holy and divine likeness, and entrusted me with the ultimate super power of love, believing I could help save the world.

Who is a magnificent God like You?

The God who promises I can return home when my days have been counted here and a new adventure will begin.

All You ask of me is to have a little faith, meet the world from the best of myself and never hold back on love—

Because You never hold back on love from me.

A most grateful amen.

WE ALL FALL SHORT OF THE GLORY OF GOD, AND
YET GOD REDEEMS US BY GRACE ANYWAY.

ROMANS 3:23

od of mercy,

My spirit suffers at the altar of the world.

My ego: the gilt calf.

Stubborn and impatient with Your timing and glory,

I become the priest of my own destiny.

I worship everything but holiness.

Before I know it, every thought and deed is focused on my own
personal needs and selfish desires instead of those of others.

It comes as no surprise when I return to You worn,
uninspired and lonely.

Soul empty.

You welcome me back into the holy of holies.

You remind me of the worthy altar of my heart,

The place where You sit ready to impart wisdom, forgive, nourish
and offer me another chance.

You anoint my forehead with a blessing and whisper,

Worship love and all will be well.

Amen.

I DO NOT AT ALL UNDERSTAND THE MYSTERY OF
GRACE — ONLY THAT IT MEETS US WHERE WE ARE
BUT DOES NOT LEAVE US WHERE IT FOUND US.

ANNE LAMOTT

y Divine,

I call out to You today from my inner chapel—

Please enter in.

Careful for my dark corners, the scattered shards of once beautiful glass that reflect life's heartbreaks and the incense of doubt that perfumes the air between us.

Light a candle at the altar of my heart.

Speak to me of Your glory plan.

Anoint me Your priestess of love.

Use all of me:

My mind, my body, my strength and my soul,

My past, present and future,

Even my brokenness, if it will help heal Your world.

I will not be afraid to touch the open wounds as You have so tenderly touched mine.

I will stir the waters, anoint with myrrh and lift my lantern high.

I'd like to go by another name: Healer.

It is what You made me for.

Finally, my life makes sense.

Amen.

THE MOST BEAUTIFUL THINGS IN THE WORLD
CANNOT BE SEEN OR TOUCHED, THEY ARE FELT
WITH THE HEART.

ANTOINE DE SAINT-EXUPÉRY

nfinite One,

Every day I stand at the intersection of the human and the holy.

An imaginary boundary separates my material existence from
my spiritual being.

It is much easier to keep my feet planted firmly
on this side of reality, consumed in my everyday responsibilities,
needs and worries.

And yet my soul yearns to transcend.

When I dare to move into the mysterious, unseen and miraculous
realm of the spirit, I experience a lightness of being—glory,
You call it—on the mystical edge.

If only I were more adventuresome in matters of the spirit.

Then maybe I wouldn't feel so weighted to this earth and would
instead float with the angels.

Amen.

GIVE US THIS DAY, LORD, OUR DAILY MIRACLE.

PAULO COELHO

oving God,

The world is imperfect.

Evil has a long leash.

Fear tries its best to usurp Your throne

And death haunts even the steeliest of hearts.

Sometimes it's difficult to keep my inner flame alight,
to duel despair with fierce hope and trust that there is
actually a plan of salvation in place.

My soul longs to believe.

I want to stake my whole being in Your court.

Every fiber of my being yearns to trust You.

Whisper to my soul, *I am your Lord, your God, and I will not
let you go until I have done what I promised.*

And I will rise courageous for another day.

I will take on Your armor of light, lift up my banner of hope
and take my place on the side of Love.

Amen.

THERE ARE ONLY TWO WAYS TO LIVE YOUR LIFE.
ONE IS AS THOUGH NOTHING IS A MIRACLE.
THE OTHER IS AS THOUGH EVERYTHING
IS A MIRACLE.

ALBERT EINSTEIN

ear God,

So often I wonder who I am, what my purpose is and
where Your path will lead me.

Although my life is measured in gains and losses,
You only take an account of my heart.

Am I walking in the direction of love or away from it?

Forgive me when I lose the holy way, carelessly let go of
Your hand, relegate You to my periphery view and allow
my fears to upset the divine balance.

Forgive me when I don't walk this planet with more reverence.

Forgive me when I could have chosen love and did not.

You have covered my life in a tapestry of blessings.

Even the setbacks You have used to impart
wisdom and evolve my soul.

Inspire in me a deeper welling of courage and reveal my resilience.

Dare me to trust You,

And I'll brave a step forward in the direction of love.

Amen.

HOPE BEGINS IN THE DARK, THE STUBBORN HOPE
THAT IF YOU JUST SHOW UP AND TRY TO DO THE
RIGHT THING, THE DAWN WILL COME. YOU WAIT
AND WATCH AND WORK: YOU DON'T GIVE UP.

ANNE LAMOTT

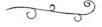

lmighty One,

When will the day come when every child on this planet
never worries about from where his or her food,
shelter and love will come?

When will the day come when cancer is obsolete and
the cancer clinics become ghost towns?

When will the day come when depression, mental illness,
addiction and loneliness are cured?

When will the day come when terrorism, persecution
and war declared in Your holy name cease?

When will the day come when the dignity of every human being
is acknowledged and appreciated?

When will the day come when families, churches,
governments and religions around the world decide
that love will be the way forward?

Your holy response: *What are you waiting for?*

Amen.

PERFECT HOPE IS ACHIEVED ON THE BRINK OF
DESPAIR WHEN, INSTEAD OF FALLING OVER THE
EDGE, WE FIND OURSELVES WALKING ON AIR.

THOMAS MERTON

od,

I am a little boat on the great sea of life.

One moment it's tangerine skies and smiles, the next ominous
clouds move in, silver rimmed in dread.

My faith quivers, rough waters batter my heart, the lightning strikes
down my courage and all I see around is darkness.

Where once I felt in control of my destiny, a theology of hope
easily upon my lips, now there is a raging squall of fear
that threatens all that I am.

I cannot help but be afraid, even angry, that You—the incarnation of
love—would place my heart in such peril.

Suddenly all is not as it seemed or should be.

I begin to question my value to You, mistrust Your power
and promises, and talk of hope feels empty words.

And then out of the wild tempest comes a voice:

I'm in the boat with you.

The storm continues to jostle my equilibrium.

But again the voice roars:

I'm in the boat with you.

Say it is true, God.

When the wind blows through my spirit, my faith trembles
within me and I've wept a sea of tears.

You will call out,

I'm in the boat with you.

Amen.

NEVER FORGET THAT LIFE CAN ONLY BE NOBLY
INSPIRED AND RIGHTLY LIVED IF YOU TAKE
IT BRAVELY AND GALLANTLY, AS A SPLENDID
ADVENTURE IN WHICH YOU ARE SETTING OUT
INTO AN UNKNOWN COUNTRY TO FACE MANY A
DANGER, TO MEET MANY A JOY, TO FIND MANY A
COMRADE, TO WIN AND LOSE MANY A BATTLE.

ANNIE BESANT

oly One,

I am Your catechumen in hope.

Although confined by the fixed boundaries of time and space,

You have given me a noble spirit and everything I would need to
live a life of profound meaning.

So hallowed, and yet so short, my stay here.

Set me free to experience how love works.

The time must be now.

Stardust my life with signs of your grace incarnating.

Whisper the secrets of the universe to me so I rest
knowing that You have a plan in place where all works
out for the good in the end.

Soften the edges of my humanity so that my divinity may shine
through and others would be drawn to You.

Open the eyes of my heart so that I don't miss the magic.

I pray for more time on this side to take in all the beauty.

Your hope has snuck into the satchel of my heart.

I shall never be the same again.

Amen.

FOR WITH GOD NOTHING WILL BE IMPOSSIBLE.

LUKE 1:37

eloved,

You stitched a luminous thread of hope into the seams of my heart
and then set me free to discover my unique destiny.

It's not until my path bends into a dark valley, I wrestle with the
angels for answers to life's tough questions or duel with the beasts
of evil, hurt, heartbreak and death—

That I question if hope is enough.

What is hope, really?

The inextinguishable light that I carry into
the dark nights of my soul?

The tender voice that rises up from a secret place and says
"I am here and I will not leave you" when life humbles?

The declaration by the Angel Gabriel,
"Nothing is impossible with God."

The promise that not my life, not my death, not my fears for today
or my worries for tomorrow, not my flaws or secret doubts will
ever separate me from You and Your eternal plan for my salvation?

It's the all of it.

Can I dare to live in hope?

Amen.

WE ALL WANT TO KNOW WHY WE ARE HERE.
WHAT IS OUR MISSION IN LIFE?
THOSE PEOPLE WHO KNOW IT ARE EASY TO SPOT:
THEIR LIVES SHINE WITH MEANING.

CAROLINE MYSS

nfinite God,

One day I awakened to the reality that joy is not
an experience of the flesh but is rooted in that
most intimate and secret place of my being.

Joy is the knowledge that You are my beginning, my middle
and my end. You called my life into being, count my days
and will take my hand at the last breath.

Joy is the confidence that when I call out, You are always there—no
matter the time, the place, the distance between us or the gravity of
my sins—ready to hear the secrets of my heart.

Joy is discovering my holy purpose and then using every remaining
breath and quivering muscle to pursue it.

Joy comes when I take the mystical leap and place my whole
being—my dreams, my fears, my tender heart—into Your hands.

Joy is the promise that ultimately,
even if I cannot see it now, all will be well.

All will be well.

Joy is not a fleeting emotion but the state of my evolving soul.

Amen.

TAKE ME, DEAR LORD, AND SET ME
IN THE DIRECTION I AM TO GO.

FLANNERY O'CONNOR

oly One,

Today I kneel before You in all my naked vulnerability and truth.

My soul craves something of the mystical and otherworldly.

I fear I have forgotten my beginnings—

Remind me again of the scent of the heavens.

I'm curious of the other side: Eternity.

There is indeed a great fear of the final crossing

And my promised transfiguration.

I worry I'm not equipped for the change
or the necessary goodbyes.

And yet my heart belonged to You long before
my stardust was enlivened with breath.

A little more time here, please.

There's still unfinished business:

I must tell every single person I love "I love you" again and again.

And then I'll take on the wings gladly.

Amen.

THE DAY OF MY SPIRITUAL AWAKENING WAS THE
DAY I SAW — AND KNEW I SAW — ALL THINGS IN
GOD AND GOD IN ALL THINGS.

MECHTHILD OF MAGDEBURG

lmighty,

If I keep speaking into the divine silence,

One day will You whisper back?

Sometimes I wonder how I am to love that which I don't fully understand.

You feel as large and mysterious and ominous as the great, dark sea,

And in the same breath, as small and intimate as to slip unnoticed through the secret door of my beating heart.

Is curiosity a trait of the faithful?

And doubt, too?

I find myself caught on the pendulum.

I swing from here to there.

From hope and a genuine desire to learn every line of Your illumined silhouette,

To fear that You are only an illusion and one day I'll turn to dust.

I want to be braver.

I want to believe that You and I are friends.

And that Your angels circle me in protection.

Whisper that You love me.

And I'll dare to dream and hope and love—

Until the day I'm permitted to see the whole of it.

Amen.

BE BETTER THAN YOURSELF.

WILLIAM FAULKNER

 y God,

I don't want You to know me by my ego,

And yet it often speaks for me.

When will I realize that I have nothing to prove—

That You hardly notice how well I cross my t's and dot my i's.

Success on this side of heaven is measured
by the geometry of my heart.

There is always an angle:

More me, less You.

Less me, more You.

Hubris or humility?

I don't want You to know me by my ego,

Only the truth of my heart.

Less me, more You.

Amen.

Every day we are engaged in a miracle
we don't even recognize.

Thich Nhat Hanh

ivine One,

Do I bear Your holy thumbprint?

Is heaven's insignia etched in secret where I cannot see it?

Do the angels know me by name?

I need to believe that my life is of more value than the scars,
the loss, the mistakes and the doubts that twist my soul
into a Gordian knot—

An invisible knot that only one with supernatural powers can
unloosen and make straight again.

I pray and then I fear.

I give and then I take.

I hope and then I despair.

I am a tangled being

In need of Your saving.

Set me free.

I'd like to do something worthy with my life to catch
Your angels attention!

Amen.

I OWE THE WORLD AND GOD A LIFE.

WILLIAM SLOANE COFFIN

od of the heavens and the earth,

What is it that You need most of me?

I fear I am missing the point.

Too soon death will tap me on the shoulder and that will be that.

There's no time to judge, to be stingy or guarded, when it comes to my participation on the side of love.

Even in the darkness,

You insist there is a ripening gospel all around, even within me.

Practice resurrection, You whisper.

It is the glory job.

Not one day can pass, business as usual.

I must be a whirling dervish, open my arms to the world

And practice resurrection.

Imagine if every day I did something that made another soul smile, believe, hope—

Rise.

Finally I understand the Miracle.

Amen.

Earth's crammed with heaven.

Elizabeth Barrett Browning

rchitect of Love,

I don't want to miss Your world shimmering.

Today I will play the role of Your priestess and bless all that I see:

The weeping willow waving her graceful arms in the wind,
encouraging me to dance in the moment.

The turtle moving ever so slowly across my path, teaching me
patience with every step.

The sage owl that stares through me from his high throne to
remind me that I have a soul.

The dappled light that triumphantly breaks through the dark,
evergreen canopy, proving Your light always finds a way.

The warmth of the sun that melts away my fears and doubts.

The cool, dark shadows that beckon me to reflect.

The pealing laughter of my 3-year-old that supernaturally
grows my heart inside my chest.

The "I love you," "I love you more," "That's impossible" goodnight
exchange between daughter and mother.

The silent benediction just before I slip into my illumined dreams,
whispering thank You for another day.

Amen.

SO EACH OF US SHALL GIVE ACCOUNT
OF HIMSELF TO GOD.

ROMANS 14:12

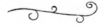

oving God,

Today I played the villain in my story.

And sadly, quite well.

I was impatient, quick to judge and unforgiving.

I thought only of myself.

I took for granted the warmth of the sun on my cheek

And turned my back cold on every opportunity to show mercy.

When I should have listened, I spoke louder.

When You tried to reach me, I feigned busyness.

How many chances did You offer me to play the hero?

A word of kindness here, an offering of hope there,
a flicker of light in a corner of despair.

Grace was mine to give.

And yet here I stand at the end of the day,

On a darkened stage, my invisible horns plain to see.

Before the curtain closes, I beg You for another day.

Amen.

WALK AS IF YOU ARE KISSING THE
EARTH WITH YOUR FEET.

THICH NHAT HANH

y Creator,

I bow to Your imagination.

I could never have conceived the awe of it:

The darkness, the light, every hue of the rainbow.

The owl's soliloquy, the regal mountain peaks, the sea laden with treasures befitting a queen, an eagle's wingspan to impress and the elegant sway of fields of wheat.

The joy and the heartbreak.

The sheer beauty and surprising challenge of it.

The mysterious power of forgiveness and the magic of grace.

A son who dies only to rise back to life.

My unique heart—entrusted with everything
I would need to save the world.

It's tremendous—the Divine imagination.

I sit in expectation of what You'll think of next.

Amen.

NO POWER IN THE SKY ABOVE OR IN THE EARTH
BELOW—INDEED, NOTHING IN ALL OF CREATION
WILL EVER BE ABLE TO SEPARATE US FROM THE
LOVE OF GOD.

ROMANS 8:39

earest God,

Handle me with tenderness today.

The world outside feels like sandpaper to my world inside.

Every fiber of my being wants to run—

From the pain, the heartbreak, the grief,

From death.

But then my life would be a mere shadow of Your dream,

Narrow and finite.

I would miss the unexpected star storms of grace.

I'm still in the cocoon,

My soul becoming.

Teach me faith.

One day I will have the courage to break free

And take the leap.

Amen.

No mud,
No lotus.

Thich Nhat Hanh

od,

You choose the most unexpected, the lost, the flawed, the broken,

To carry out Your divine bidding here on earth.

Abraham, Moses, King David, St. Peter and Paul, the Marys—

It's revelatory

And frightening.

Because it means You might choose me,

Lowly me,

To do something noble, courageous, kind and loving.

Give me a sign and I will give a piece of my heart to every single person who crosses my path,

Until I show up at Your door empty handed,

Love spent.

Finally, my life will serve a higher purpose.

Amen.

FOR EVERYTHING THERE IS A SEASON, AND A TIME
FOR EVERY MATTER UNDER HEAVEN.

ECCLESIASTES 3:1

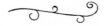

oly One,

Time is slipping through my fingers.

How many years I didn't even notice the hourglass at work.

I falsely believed that Time was my friend.

Until the goodbyes, so many of them:

To my innocence and rosy youth, to yet another spring and winter come and gone, to holding a baby close to my breast, to the musical score of little feet now grown, to those whom I loved who left me for heaven, to my invincible body and steel-trap mind.

How did it all go by so fast?

So much beautiful living,

Now memories tucked deep in the velvet envelope of my heart.

I don't want to live in fear of the inevitable.

One day the world will say goodbye to me, too.

Until then,

I'll not waste a granule.

Amen.

SEE GOD IN ALL THINGS AND
ALL WILL BE RIGHT IN THE WORLD.

St. Ignatius of Loyola

 nfinite One,

Instead of looking for life's answers,

I'm going to look for You, my God, in all and everything.

Curiosity will be my compass.

I'll keep my fears in check.

Be daring.

My mantra: No regrets.

Blood, sweat, tears and laughter.

Love will be my religion.

I'm going to wear out my welcome here on earth.

Show up at heaven's door,

My humanity in tatters,

Not a stone left uncovered or bottle uncorked,

Hugged every moment.

Given You my all and more.

At the bell tolling, I'd like to hear You say,

That was a life worth My breath.

Amen.

HOPE...IS AN ORIENTATION OF THE SPIRIT, AN
ORIENTATION OF THE HEART; IT TRANSCENDS THE
WORLD THAT IS IMMEDIATELY EXPERIENCED AND
IS ANCHORED SOMEWHERE BEYOND ITS HORIZONS.
IT IS NOT A CONVICTION THAT ALL WILL TURN
OUT WELL, BUT THE CERTAINTY THAT ALL WILL
MAKE SENSE, REGARDLESS OF HOW IT TURNS OUT.

VÁCLAV HAVEL

lmighty One,

Is the Darkness winning?

Suicide bombers rage, strange viruses spread, children go hungry,
drugs destroy, depression casts a long shadow
and global warming is stealing away our Eden.

It's enough to throw up the white flag.

I don't want to give in to the anxiety.

I still hope on hope

That heaven will flood in.

In the meantime, what can I do?

I will lift up my lantern,

And maybe another will follow my lead.

And another.

Suddenly what was once dark is now light.

Hope unleashed.

And Your love makes headway.

Amen.

I HAVE RAISED YOU UP FOR THE VERY PURPOSE OF
SHOWING MY POWER IN YOU, SO THAT MY NAME
MAY BE PROCLAIMED IN ALL THE EARTH.

ROMANS 9:17

ivine,

You know me like not even I know me,

The puzzle that I am,

The smooth and the jagged.

Maybe I can hide behind a smile to the world but not to You.

My secrets are plain to the divine eye.

You are privy to my inner conversation,

Sometimes worthy, often not.

You know my insecurities

And can count the number of times I have
betrayed my heart for the status quo.

You know me,

The divided life I lead,

My struggle to fit in the world,

Without losing my true north.

My soul longs to be a saint, my ego a queen.

I'm a work in progress.

And You are my patient friend, helping me along.

Maybe one day all my pieces will find their right place,

And finally I will be whole.

Amen.

He restores my soul.

Psalm 23:3

oving God,

Your Holy Spirit percolates in my marrow,
lighting me from the inside out.

So why do I wrestle with the angels when
the Holy Grail is within my grasp?

Loosen the bindings of fear so that hope
may catch me in its luminous net.

School me on how to reach down into my divine depths,
the place of my noble soul, to rediscover:

A welling of courage that I thought not possible.

A capacity for love that makes even me heroic.

A supernatural peace beyond my own understanding.

And a flicker of light, heaven's guarantee:

The darkness shall not take me.

Amen.

WHEN THE TRAIN GOES THROUGH A TUNNEL
AND THE WORLD GOES DARK, DO YOU JUMP OUT?
OF COURSE NOT. YOU SIT STILL AND TRUST THE
ENGINEER TO GET YOU THROUGH.

CORRIE TEN BOOM

ather in heaven,

Do You just shake Your head when You gaze upon me?

When will I get out of Your way?

You want to save me,

But I have to be willing to be saved.

I cannot face this life on my own.

Not one breath of it.

The gospel truth:

You were the first to love me,

And You will be the last.

I must turn myself over

And let You have Your way with me.

Here I am,

A lump of clay in divine hands.

Eternally Yours.

Amen.

INTO THE SILENT NIGHT
AS WE MAKE OUR WEARY WAY
WE KNOW NOT WHERE,
JUST WHEN THE NIGHT BECOMES ITS DARKEST
AND WE CANNOT SEE OUR PATH,
JUST THEN
IS WHEN THE ANGELS RUSH IN,
THEIR HANDS FULL OF STARS.

ANN WEEMS

od,

Every time my heart breaks,

I imagine the heavens open up angry

And weep a tempest.

The winged take to the skies seeking solace from the stars.

The haloed drop to their knees in solemn prayer.

The Son paces his throne room in the clouds.

The Holy Spirit collects my every tear into her glass bottle.

While You, the Almighty, set about putting me back together

Ever so tenderly.

Because that is what Love does.

Amen.

FOR ME, PRAYER IS THE HEART'S IMPULSE, A
SIMPLE GAZE TOWARD HEAVEN. IT IS A CRY OF
GRATITUDE AND LOVE FROM THE DEPTH OF TRIAL
AS WELL AS THE HEIGHT OF GLORY. FINALLY, IT IS
SOMETHING GREAT, SUPERNATURAL, THAT
EXPANDS MY SOUL AND UNITES ME TO JESUS.

ST. THÉRÈSE OF LISIEUX

allowed One,

I stand in awe and wonder at Your daring plan of love.

Just when I begin to despair, Your light rises up
and defeats my darkness.

Heaven breaks through.

Resurrection, the business of God.

Death is not the victor, only love the hero.

Your Son now goes by a new name: Savior.

His scent of hope is potent.

Glory shimmers beneath the cloak of my humanity.

I will fall headlong into grace.

It is a love story.

Our story.

How do I begin to thank You?

On bended knee, I offer the only thing of value:

My heart.

Alleluia!

Acknowledgements

Augustine, Saint. *The Confessions of St. Augustine.* Trans. John K. Ryan. New York: Image Books, 1960. Print.

Berry, Wendell. *Given.* Berkeley: Counterpoint, 2006. Print.

Brooks, Noah. Harpers Weekly. July 1865.

Browning, Elizabeth Barrett. *Aurora Leigh.* Ed. Kerry McSweeney. Oxford: Oxford University Press, 2008. Print.

Buechner, Frederick. *Listening to Your Life: Daily Meditations With Frederick Buechner.* New York: HarperOne, 1992. Print.

"Be Still." The Work of the People. Web. 29 June 2016.

Cannon, Master Charles. *"Paradise Is at Your Own Center."* Synchronicity Foundation. Web. 27 June 2016.

Coelho, Paulo. *Manuscript Found in Accra.* Trans. Margaret Jull Costa. New York: Vintage Books, 2013. Print.

Coffin, William Sloane. *Credo.* Louisville: WJK Press, 2004. Print.

Das, Lama Surya. *Awakening to the Sacred: Creating a Personal Spiritual Life.* New York: Harmony Books, 2000. Print.

d'Avila, Saint Teresa. *Interior Castle.* Trans. E. Allison Peers. Mineola: Dover Publications, 2007. Print.

Dellinger, David. *From Yale to Jail: The Life Story of a Moral Dissenter.* New York: Pantheon, 1993. Print.

de Saint-Exupéry, Antoine. *The Little Prince.* Trans. Richard Howard. Geneva: Houghton Mifflin Harcourt, 2000. Print.

Dillard, Annie. *Pilgrim at Tinker Creek.* New York: Harper Perennial Modern Classics, 2013. Print.

Egan, Harvey D. *An Anthology of Christian Mysticism.* Yonkers: Pueblo Books, 1991. Print.

Faulkner, William. *"The Art of Fiction, No. 12."* Interview with Jean Stein. The Paris Review, Spring 1956, no. 12. Web. 6 July 2016.

"A Feather on the Breath of God." St. Hildegard of Bingen. Hyperion Records Limited. Web. 29 June 2016.

Foster, Richard J. *Prayer: Finding the Heart's True Home.* New York: HarperCollins, 1992. Print.

Franck, Frederick. *Messenger of the Heart: The Book of Angelus Silesius.* Bloomington: World Wisdom, 2005. Print.

"The Gnostic Gospels." The Nag Hammadi Library in English. Elaine Pagels. New York: Vintage Books, 1979. xiii-xxiii. Print. The Gnostic Society Library. Web. June 20, 2016.

Graham, Linda. *Bouncing Back: Rewiring Your Brain for Maximum Resilience and Well-Being.* San Francisco: New World Library, 2013. Print.

Hanh, Thich Nhat. *Moments of Mindfulness: Daily Inspiration.* Berkeley: Parallax Press, 2013. Print.

Hanh, Thich Nhat. *No Mud, No Lotus: The Art of Transforming Suffering.* Berkeley: Parallax Press, 2014. Print.

Hanh, Thich Nhat. *Peace Is Every Step: The Path of Mindfulness in Everyday* Life. Ed. Arnold Kotler. New York: Bantam Books, 1992. Print.

Haskins, Henry. *Meditations in Wall Street.* New York: William Morrow & Company, 1940. Print.

Havel, Václav. *Disturbing the Peace: A Conversation with Karel Huizdala.* New York: Vintage Books, 1991. Print.

Holy Bible, Revised Standard Version. Nashville: Thomas Nelson and Sons, 1952. Print.

Irenaeus, Saint. *Against Heresies.* Veritatis Splendor Publications, 2012. Print.

Kasimow, Harold, ed. *No Religion Is an Island: Abraham Joshua Heschel and Interreligious Dialogue.* Eugene: Wipf and Stock Publishers, 2009. Print.

Lamott, Anne. *Bird by Bird: Some Instructions on Writing and Life.* New York: Anchor Books, 1995. Print.

Lamott, Anne. *Traveling Mercies: Some Thoughts on Faith.* New York: Anchor Books, 2000. Print.

Laozi. *Tao Te Ching.* New York: Harper Perennial, 1994. Print.

Levertov, Denise. *The Collected Poems of Denise Levertov.* New York: New Directions, 2013. Print.

Loeb, Paul Rogat, ed. *The Impossible Will Take a Little While: A Citizen's Guide to Hope in a Time of Fear.* New York: Basic Books, 2004. Print.

Lucado, Max. *Safe in the Shepherd's Arms.* Nashville: J. Countryman, 2002. Print.

Martin, SJ, James. *My Life With the Saints.* Chicago: Loyola Press, 2006. Print.

Star, Jonathan, trans. *Rumi: In the Arms of the Beloved.* New York: TarcherPerigree, 2008. Print.

Mason, Farrell. *"I Know Myself Because You Know Me."* Bread and Honey, 29 Sept 2013. Web. 27 June 2016.

McFague, Sallie. *A New Climate for Theology: God, the World, and Global Warming.* Minneapolis: Fortress Press, 2008. Print.

Merton, Thomas. *A Book of Hours.* Notre Dame: Sorin Books, 2007. Print.

Merton, Thomas. *Life and Holiness.* Martino Fine Books, 2013. Print.

Merton, Thomas. *No Man Is an Island.* Geneva: Mariner Books, 2002. Print.

Myss, Caroline. *Sacred Contracts: Awakening Your Divine Potential.* New York: Harmony Books, 2003. Print.

Nicholson, Reynold A. *The Mystics of Islam.* Bloomington: World Wisdom, 2003. Print.

Nouwen, Henri J.M. *The Return of the Prodigal Son: A Story of Homecoming.* New York: Image Books, 1994. Print.

O'Connor, Flannery. *A Prayer Journal.* Ed. W.A. Sessions. New York: Farrar, Straus & Giroux, 2013. Print.

Oliver, Mary. *Evidence.* Boston: Beacon Press, 2010. Print.

Oliver, Mary. *Owls and Other Fantasies: Poems and Essays.* Boston: Beacon Press, 2006. Print.

Plato. *Plato: Five Dialogues.* Ed. John M. Cooper. Trans. G.M.A. Grube. Indianapolis: Hackett Publishing Company, 2002. Print.

Teresa, Mother. *No Greater Love.* San Francisco: New World Library, 2002. Print.

"The Prayer of the Heart." Orthodox Prayer. Web. 26 June 2016.

"Pray Like the Bush Is Burning." Two Minutes of Grace, 28 Sept 2012. Web. 26 June 2016.

Rilke, Rainer Maria. *Rilke's Book of Hours: Love Poems to God.* New York: Riverhead Books, 2005. Print.

Rumi, Jelaluddin. *Love Is a Stranger: Selected Lyric Poetry of Jelaluddin Rumi.* Boulder: Shambhala Publications, 2000. Print.

Rohr, Richard. *Falling Upward: A Spirituality for the Two Halves of Life.* Hoboken: Jossey-Bass, 2011. Print.

Stevens, Becca. *Find Your Way Home: Words From the Street, Wisdom From the Heart.* Nashville: Abingdon Press, 2008. Print.

"St. Patrick's Breastplate Prayer." The Prayer Foundation. Web. 26 June 2016.

Tozer, A.W. *The Pursuit of God.* CreateSpace, 2012. Print.

Vasudevan, Mudalodu. *Emotional Stress.* London: JP Medical Publishers, 2003. Print.

Vaughan-Lee, Llewellyn. *Prayer of the Heart in Christian and Sufi Mysticism.* Point Reyes Station: Golden Sufi Center, 2012. Print.

"Verse (2:115) – English Translation." The Quranic Arabic Corpus. Web. 27 June 2016.

Walsch, Neale Donald. *"Your Life Is Your Prayer."* The Power of Prayer: Writings on Prayer. Ed. Dale Salwak. San Francisco: New World Library, 1999. Print.

Weems, Ann. *Kneeling in Bethlehem.* Louisville: Westminster John Knox Press, 1987. Print.

Wilde, Oscar. *The Ballad of Reading Gaol.* Hertfordshire: Wordsworth Editions, 1999. Print.

Williams, Nancy. *A Penny for Your Thoughts.* Epitome Books, 2009. Print.

Williamson, Marianne. *Illuminata: A Return to Prayer.* New York: Riverhead Books, 1995. Print.

arrell Mason lives in Nashville, Tennessee with her husband and six children. She has a Master of Arts degree from the University of Manchester and Sotheby's London and is currently finishing her Master of Divinity at Vanderbilt University. She is the author of *Alma Gloria and the Olive Tree* and *The Angel and the Raven*.

Farrell is passionate about raising funds, awareness and especially hope for kids with cancer. A portion of proceeds from all of her writings go to Memorial Sloan Kettering in New York and Vanderbilt Children's Hospital in Nashville in honor of her son.

You can follow Farrell and enjoy her weekly blog posts at

www.breadandhoneyblog.net.

CPSIA information can be obtained
at www.ICGtesting.com
Printed in the USA
LVOW11*0409011017
550592LV00001B/3/P